This study is whole heartedly dedicated ‘ The Almighty’ and my lovable husband, son and my parents and brothers and sisters. I thank Almighty' for mentally guided me in every way. All of these i indebtedly dedicated.

FEMININE EXISTENTIALISM AND SOCIO PSYCHOLOGY IN THE SELECTED NOVELS OF ANITA DESAI.

MRS. EMILY RANI. S

Contents

ACKNOWLEDGEMENTS

I'm deeply indepted to Dr. Vijayaraghavan, Associate Professor of English, Nehru Arts and Science College, coimbatore. For his continuous and valuable support and guidance to complete this work. My special thanks my loving husband who supported me mentally and financially to successfully made this attempt to complete this work. My heartiest thanks to all my family members who supported me behind this work.

About The Author

Prof. Emily Rani has been a dynamic professor for more than 20 years of teaching. She hold her degrees, duly in under graduate in literature, post graduate in literature, and she did her preliminary research in American literature. She did her degress at coimbatore Government college of Arts and Science, Coimbatore. She had a wide experience for guiding students for projects and research papers. And without any doubt this book would make the budding readers more and interested in visiting the wonderful world of Anitha Desai.

I

INTRODUCTION

In today's world, we have to get knowledge of advanced technologies and all kinds of branches of Science. There is an urgent need of such a common language which can be understood by youth all over India and the language in which all data and information is available. India is a vast country with different languages in different parts of the country. These regional languages differ from each other so much that it is not possible to communicate with people of other regions without a common language. Further, India is growing on all fronts whether it is social or economic angle.

India is on the road to become a strong and prosperous nation in the world. India is trying to maintain a good foreign policy. For all this, there is need of a common language i.e., English. It is this language which is understood almost all over the region in addition to the national language Hindi. All schools and colleges teach English and mostly have it as the medium of instruction.

India is a one nation, it is a country with unity in diversity. We speak a dozens of different languages. For people belonging to different states, a common language is essential to communicate with each other and that is English. Further, a nation can remain intact only when its leaders can understand the people living in different regions and can communicate with them in effective and cordial manner. All leaders cannot understand more than three to five languages of various regions. However, they can easily understand the common language English. This language is important to inspire unity not only at the national level but also at the international level. To curb the separatist tendencies of our varied communities, we must continue to teach English. To survive in modern society, English knowledge is as essential as water.

In India, English serves two purposes. First, it provides a linguistic tool for the administrative cohesiveness of the country, causing people who speak different languages to become united. Secondly, it serves as a language of wider communication, including a large variety of different people covering a vast area. It overlaps with local languages in certain spheres of influence and in public domains. Generally, English is used among Indians as a 'link' language and it is the first language for many well-educated Indians. It is also the second language for many who speak more than one language in India.

After Independence, India became a nation state, and it was intended that English would gradually be phased out as the language of administration. But there was no simple solution as to which language should replace it. At first Hindi, the most widely spoken language, seemed the obvious choice, but following violent protests in 1963 in the state of Tamil Nadu against the imposition of Hindi as a national language, opinion has remained divided. In a country with over 900 million people and more than a thousand languages, it is difficult to choose a single national language, as mother tongue speakers of that language would automatically enjoy greater social status and have easier access to positions of power and influence.

Indian writing in English has a relatively short but highly charged history .It started with the advent of East India Company in India. It all started in the summer of 1608 when Emperor Jahangir, in the courts of Mughals, welcomed Captain William Hawkins, Commander of British Naval Expedition ,Hector. It was India's first tryst with an Englishman and English. Jahangir later allowed Britain to open a permanent port and factory on the special request of King James IV that was conveyed by his ambassador Sir Thomas Roe. English were here to stay.

In its early stages, the Indian writings in English were heavily influenced by the Western art form of the novel. It was typical for the early Indian English language writers to use English unadulterated by Indian words to convey experiences that were primarily Indian. The core reason behind this step was the fact that most of the readers were either British or British educated Indians. In the coming century, the writings were largely confined to writing history chronicles and government gazettes.

In the early 20th century, when the British conquest of India was achieved, a new breed of writers started to emerge on the block. These writers were essentially British who were born or brought up or both in India. Their writing consisted of Indian themes and sentiments but the way of storytelling was primarily western.. This group consisted likes of Rudyard Kipling, Jim Corbett and George Orwell among others. Books such as *Kim, The JungleBook, 1984, Animal Farm* and *The man-eaters of Kumaon* etc were liked and read all over the English-speaking world. In fact, some of the writings of that era are still considered to be the masterpieces of English Literature. In those periods, natives were represented by the likes of Rabindra Nath Tagore and Sarojini Naidu. In fact, *Geetanjali* helped Tagore win Nobel Prize for Literature in the year 1913

The East India Company spread its wings in southern peninsula and English language started to get newer pockets of influence. But it was still time for the first English book to capitalize. Late 17th century saw the coming of printing press in India but the publications were largely confined to either printing Bible or government decrees. Then came newspapers. It was in 1779 that the first English Newspaper named Hickey's Bengal Gazette was published in India. The breakthrough in Indian English literature came in 1793 A.D. when a person by the name of Sake Dean Mahomet published a book in London titled *Travels of Dean Mahomet*. This was essentially Mahomet's travel narrative that can be put somewhere between a Non-Fiction and a Travelogue.

In 1793, Sake Dean Mahomed wrote perhaps the first book by an Indian in English, called *The Travels of Dean Mahomed*. However, most early Indian writing in English was non-fictional work, such as biographies and political essays. Recognition of the country as one in the world community increased Indian writers' self confidence, and they assumed the role of critics both of past and present instead of merely voicing his times, as the previous writers had done. This began to change in the late 1800s, when famous Indian authors who wrote mostly in their mother tongue, began to try their hand at writing in English. In the early 1900s, Rabindranath Tagore began translating his works from Bengali to English.

Ever since the publication of Bankim Chandra Chaterjee's novel *Rajmohan's Wife* in1864, the Indian novel in English has grown by leaps and bounds in respect of bulk, variety and maturity. After the World War I, the Indian English novel became determinedly more realistic and less idealized. Soon after, a new generation of Indian authors, who wrote almost exclusively in English, hit the bookshelves, beginning in 1935 with R.K. Narayan's *Swami and Friends* and Mulk Raj Anand's *Untouchable.* Raja Rao's *Kanthapura* followed in 1938.they were known as 'The Big Three'. They shaped the destiny of Indian English fiction. What made Narayan's, Anand's and Rao's writing different from the Indian authors before them was that their stories were about the contemporary man on the street. There was also an Indianness to their work, in terms of the words they used and their style of writing. This resonated with the new, but growing ranks of Indians reading English literature. Their works were the forerunners to the magnificent diversity of Indian writing in English that we see today.

Social realism is the major concern in his works. He has brought innovations in fiction by making an untouchable the hero or anti-hero of his first novel, *Untouchable.* Anand takes characters from contemporary life who have been deprived of their rights by the oppressors. His Marxist leanings are unmistakable. A person who lived more than twenty years abroad during his youth, unlike the contemporary diasporic writers was never in search of 'home'. 'Home' was uppermost in his mind and deeply engraved in his heart. Hence, he never lost touch with Indian reality and social conditions. Of Anand's fiction, Anna Rutherford writes: "Anand's characters invariably fall into three classes: the victims who are usually the protagonists; the oppressors, those who oppose change and progress, and the goodmen." (R.K.Rarayan's Novels: A mix of Myth and Reality, P 145)

Feminism is a collection of movements and ideologies aimed at defining, establishing and defending equal political, economic and social rights for women. French Philosopher Charles Fourier is credited with having originated the word in 1837. It is a global and revolutionary ideology as well as a socio-cultural movement that aims at the freedom of woman from male domination in the patriarchal society. It highlights various hidden and oppressive aspects of man – woman relationship. It has a profound impact on the debate concerning the relation between genders, culture and creativity and knocks down the claims of certain cultures, which believe that woman can only produce children and not art.

The rise of Feminism as a movement on the continent began with the crucial question that portrayal of women by male artists must be deficient for; even the most imaginative of male writers is by no means equipped to give an authentic rendering of the female sensibility. Of late there has been a tendency among the women Indian novelists writing in English to share this view. There has emerged a group of women novelists who try to give their own side of the story from their own point of view. Traditionally Indian women have been treated as marginalized lot. They were represented as spineless, wooden creature, subjected to male domination. The laws of Manu dictated the position of women in the family and society. Women were never allowed to be independent and had to spend life under the authority of a man. The sublimation and suppression of natural desires and aspirations creates a deep struggle in women. The position of women has always been reflected in the novels written by Indian women writers in English. They capture the intricacies of the problems of women caught between the two worlds of tradition and modernity.

Mostly, they deal with women's suffering and the pathetic plight of women under male domination. The first category of feminist writers consists of writers like Jane Austen, Bronte Sisters and others. The second category includes writers like Emily Dickinson, Virginia Woolf, Sylvia Plath and many others. The first category of writers have struggled to be simply acknowledged by the intelligentia while the second group has revolted against the male oriented society and sought to establish an isolated world away from the males. The third group has maintained a balance between the above two extremes by being both feminine and feminist at the same time. This group of writers have also less talked about the social or political freedom and never visualized a world existing without men. Kamala Das is a part of this third category. The emergence of women novelists in Indian English literature took place as early as the last quarter of the nineteenth century. But, it was only after independence, that they could make solid contribution to Indian English fiction. The post-Independence period, has brought to the forefront a number of noted women novelists who have enriched Indian English fiction by a creative release of feminine sensibility. The woman has been the focus of many literary works in this period.

Writers like Kamala Markandaya, Nayantara Sahgal, Ruth Prawer Jhabvala, Anita Desai and Shashi Deshpande have achieved recognision of recent times. Anita Desai like Joyce and Woolf is widely recognized as the pioneer of psychological novel in modern Indian English literature. She penetrates psychologically deep into the inner working of women and externalizes their passive reaction. In his respect she approximates to Dostoevsky, Proust, Virginia

Woolf, James Joyce and Henry James.

Born in Mussoorie on the 24th june 1937 of mixed parentage a Bengali father and a German mother, she was to be benefited by the diverse influences which led to the fermentation of her poetic imagination. At a tender age of seven, she began to write prose, and published some small pieces in children's magazine. She had her education-first at Queen Mary's school, and then at Miranda House, Delhi University, where she took her Bachelor's degree in English literature in 1957.

Anita Desai has several books to her credit which include *Cry, the Peacock* (1963), *Voices in the City* (1965), *Bye-Bye Blackbird* (1971), *Where shall we go this summer?* (1975), *Fire on the Mountain* (1977), (for which she won Royal Society of Literature's of Letters Award, *The Village by the Sea* (1982) *In Custody* (1984), (which was short listed for the 1984 Booker Prize). *Baumgartner's Bombay* (1988) and her latest novel *Journey To Ithaca*. Desai's short stories have been collected under the title *Games of Twilight* (1978). Besides these novels, her review articles and interviews are considered to be the epitomes of fictional interest and flavour.

Desai's characters are intense, self absorbed, even morbidly so, possessed by a conscience that never allows them peace of mind, constantly analyzing, probing and questioning, merciless in its passion for introspection. In *Where Shall We Go This Summer*, Anita follows the track of Bronte sisters, who chose to study the heart and mind of women's point of view. Their novels provide glimpses into the tortured souls of their heroines. In like manner Anita too portrays the tragic intensity of her women characters with a feminist perspective. The novel *Where Shall We Go This Summer* depicts the tragic life of Sita who leads a life of isolation and loneliness in her husband's house. Her unmitigated suffering drives her to a state of madness and desperation.

In Anita Desai's *Bye- Bye,Black Bird* the western figure Sarah marries an Indian working in London. Sarah living on two different planes playing two roles, struggles for an indentity leaving her in a state of loneliness. Cultural alienation place a vital role in this novel. Anita Desai has added a new dimension to Indo-Anglian fiction by concentrating on the exploration of the troubled psyche of her characters, especially, the women in particular. The women writers in Indo-Anglian fiction have shown greater understanding and strength to dig deep into the psyche of the Indian characters. She has depicted through her characters, feminine personality and feminine psyche better than other Indo-Anglian novelists.

II

WHERE SHALL WE GO THIS SUMMER

Man and wife do not, as a rule, live together they only breakfast together, dine together, and sleep in the same room. In most cases the woman knows nothing of the man's working life and he knows nothing of her working life (he calls it her home life) (Bernard Shaw, Prefaces-11).

Anita Desai is one of the major voices in modern Indian English fiction, K.R. Shrinivasa Iyengar stated. The first two novels of Anita Desai Cry, *the Peacock* and *voices in the city* have added a new dimension to the achievement of the Indian women writers in English. This dimension takes multiple forms.(IWE, P 64)

If Maya suffers from Psychological alienation and Sarah from cultural alienation, the sense of alienation experienced by Sita, *in Where Shall We Go This Summer*, is difficult to explain. Sita, the protagonist is a married woman in her forties, a mother of four children, pregnant for the fifth time, living in a Bombay flat with her husband Raman, an upper middle class factory owner. The novel *Where Shall We Go This Summer* (1975) deals with a distracted wife looking to break out her matrimony. The plot follows Sita as she arrives on the pastoral island of Manori after a twenty year absence. She has brought along two of her four children, having abandoned the others with her businessman - husband in their home in Bombay. In the third trimester of yet another pregnancy and convinced that the world is hopelessly nurtured by cruelty and violence, Sita has returned to the island because she believes that it possesses magical powers which can safely terminate her pregnancy.

Her quixotic wish is that she should keep it safely in her womb and prevent it from being born into this wicked world. Raman is unable to understand her unusual idea. Their level of understanding is not the same. Raman is pragmatic and outspoken whereas Sita is an introvert. Sita is a sensitive woman very much alive to the happenings around her, the cruel violence, that she finds in the human and non-human world around her. She suffers from the existential predicament. Women's writing continues to occupy a place of importance for more reasons than one. It projects the responses of more than half of humanity and reflects a consciousness constructed by gender. Women's writing has questioned the existing viewpoints which are essentially patriarchal. All women's writing need not necessarily be feminist. But feminist interpretations can emerge through absence and negation. The sufferings of Indian women, marital disharmony, existentialism, anger, dual tradition are the major themes of feminist writing. Female quest for identity has been a pet theme for many a woman novelist.

Marital discord recurs as the theme of the novels of Anita Desai. Her novels, with a touch of feminist concern, portray the failed marriage relationship which often leads to alienation and loneliness of the characters. Her novels, like, *Cry, the Peacock, Where Shall We Go This Summer, Voices in the City,* and *Bye-Bye, Blackbird* also deal with the theme of alienation and emotional stress. Sita's character is analyzed through three different parts of the novel. Part one describes her present life. She is vexed of her husband's passive behavior. She considers the world wicked and be hopeful of escaping from the hasty surroundings. She doesn't like her fifth baby born and face these destructions. With these musings of keeping the baby unborn, she leaves the urban house and goes to the magic land.

Manori with her children Menaka and Karan. Part two deals with the past – Sita's life at Manori. She remembers her life in Manori before twenty years. She remembers her life before marriage. Everybody had great respect in her father. He set an ashram in his house and many followed his ideals. He is a saint to his disciples and a magic man to the villagers. Part three, the final part shows her coming back. It analyzes her mental state by drawing a parallel between her fancies and the reality. Her children who were accustomed to the urban life could not adjust in the island. Her daughter writes a letter to her father and they go back to Bombay. The significant thing throughout the novel is Sita's wisdom. Despite the tensed moments she has always been conscious of her surroundings. Her insightful movements made her achieve the right path. Sita could not even treat her husband's friends, guests, and visitors with tolerance. They appeared to her like animals. Later she could analyze the contrast, the life in Bombay and her imaginary world. She says, "I should have known how to channel my thoughts and feelings, how to put them to use. I should have given my life some shape then some meaning.

When she remembers her childhood, she remembers how she used to live in her small world which had given her solace – being an escape from her inabilities. This skill of analyzing situation shows her matured self perceived later. Her responsible nature is observed when she thought of taking care of her children on her own, despite the hallucinations, loneliness and restlessness in her existence. In this novel, Sita's own attitude to married life must have been warped by the knowledge and experiences in regard to their parents. The cause of her unhappiness is rooted in the miserable and lonely childhood. Her mother ran away to Benares leaving her husband and children behind and gave no information about herself. She was deprived of her mother's affection and her father also failed to look after his children.

Moreover, his incestuous attraction for Sita's elder step-sister Rekha must have shocked and the disclosure that Rekha is not her real sister also gives her upset. Thus we see that the claim of intuition and the process of reason are at clash in *Where Shall We Go This Summer*. Forty- five - year old Sita is the mother of four children and pregnant with a fifth. But the vital link, the mother is missing in her. She desperately tries to belong to something but is isolated. Sita's crazy refusal to bring her fifth child indicates her despair. It grows out of the fear that the outer reality will crush her existence. She loses her inner identity which excludes her from all meaningful rationality. She feels that by escaping to the island of her childhood she will be able to carry out her mission. So she goes to the island of Manori .

In *Where Shall We Go This Summer,* Sita shifts from compliance to rebellion and then to withdrawal, again coming back to compliance. Since she oscillates between her changing strategies, her behavior is inconsistent and leaves much scope for disparity between her thinking and actions. In the first part of the novel, entitled *Monsoon* 67, she rebels against her family and decides to go to Manori "What I'm doing is trying to escape from the madeness here, escape to a place where it might be possible to be same again" (35) – The second part *winter* 47 depicts Sita's life twenty years back, her life with her father.This part enables us to understand her later conflicts. Alternatively, her resigned and aggressive trends dominate the third section *Monsoon* 67 (106).

Sita's husband, Raman is the son of her father's friend (a situation similar to Maya & Gautama). When Sita's father died, Raman took her from the island, sent her to college, and – because it was inevitable- married her. As she recollects, when Raman came to take her away, he closed the theatrical era of her life and led her – out of the ruined theatre – into the thin sunlight of the ordinary, the everyday, the empty and the meaningless life. It is in those terms – "empty" and "meaningless" that she views her married life from which she derives no satisfaction. The temperamental incompatibility between Raman & Sita is brought out through a number of incidents in the novel. Raman, for instance, sees no meaning in Sita trying desperately to save a wounded eagle from the crows: "They've made a good job of your eagle' said her husband, coming out with his morning cup of tea. He laughed and asked her to look at the feathers sticking out of that crow's beak. She cried that perhaps it flew away, knowing it had not.

In this novel too the central character Sita is a free but isolated individual who is solely responsible for her own actions and reactions. This way, *Where Shall We Go This Summer* deals with the facts of the life and explores the sensibility of Sita. Sita is physically unimpressive and over – sensitive. Her over-sensitiveness does not allow her to mingle with an ordinary life. It compels her to go away from this burdensome and crowded area. Sita decides to flee to Manori where there is no crowd except natural scenery. Her over – sensitiveness does not allow her to give birth to her fifth child. She wishes to say a positive, no. But her stay at Manori helps her to understand that she cannot live forever on a make believe stage and that she has to accept her existence as a whole. Sita, the protagonist of this novel like the legendary Sita, had spent many crucial years of her life on the island of her childhood, Manori. The modern Raman, unlike the legendary Raman does not understand his wife. The marital discord of the modern Rama and Sita is ironically referred with that of the idealized relationship that existed between the legendary Rama and Sita even though the similarity in names and situations is clearly seen as accidental.

Marriage does not seem to offer Raman and Sita any solution rather aggravate the situation severely. They lead their life like an ill-assorted couple by lacking altogether in harmony in their lives and their marriage bond is proved to be unions of incompatibility. Sita feels herself to be a prisoner in a house which offers her nothing but a crust of dull actions and of hopeless disappointment. Living with her rational husband, she finds her surroundings too unpleasant and cruel to cope with. Her reactions like smoking, abusing her children for trifles and getting extremely angry when the servants talk in the kitchen shows her hypersensitivity. She then decides foolishly not to give birth to the fifth child in a world of violence and develops hatred for the world. She cries and says, "I don't want to have the baby" (30). She further says, "I mean I want to keep it. I don't want it to be born in this desolate and overly meaningless world"(31). Madhusudan Prasad observes that this novel deals: "A recurrent existential theme that lies bare in the agonized modern sensibility of an Indian woman" (25).

The interrogation used as the title of the novel, *Where Shall We Go This Summer* leaves a big question mark. The name itself is suggestive of an escape from the summer that stands for the raging inner tension, frustration, disappointment, mental discord and disharmony of the inner consciousness of Sita. Anita Desai views the violence through the eyes of a woman in the limited area of her domestic relationship. Desai concludes this novel with Sita's recovery from her plunge into existential reality. Sita as a "broken bird" of the seashore analyzes the cause of her anxiety and neurotic behavior and learns to cultivate the art of survival in the destined life. Her triumph over her illusions renders the island devoid of its powers and miracles

The study of isolation experienced by women in male dominated society is a significant modern trend. In the Indian society woman are not allowed to play any active role in decision-making. They are ignored or brushed aside. In such situation Anita Desai tries to focus on the predicament of women in the society. Most of the women created by Anita Desai have some trait or the other which psychologists would love to analyse. They strikingly appear as individuals and gradually get subsumed as types of women in conflict with their environment. Such types of women are ubiquitous. Desai's mother characters are not traditional, self effacing women. Sita for instance, revolutionizes the concept of motherhood by refusing to give birth to her child in a hostile world. Preoccupation with the fragmentation of reality and its impact on the human psyche is of continued interest to Desai in all her major works. She tries to explore and convey truth which she associates with the mind and not with the body. She distinguishes clearly between truth and reality.

Anita Desai is specially noted for her sensitive portrayal of the inner life of the female characters. Several of Desai's novels explore tensions among family members and the alienation of middle-class women. She explores the intricate facts of human experience bearing upon the central experience of psychic tensions of characters. Her chief concern is human relationship. Her central theme is the existential predicament of an individual which she projects through incompatible couples – very sensitive wives and ill matched husbands. Thus, Anita Desai's female characters go through traumatic experiences in their incompatible martial bonds that push them into an emotional deprivation. The women of Desai's novels seek a serene state of loneliness in order to fly away from the suffocation that the society impels on them.

In this novel, Desai follows the track of Bronte sisters, who chose to study the heart and mind of women from women's point of view. These novels provide glimpses into the tortured souls of their heroins. In like manner Anita too portrays the tragic intensity of her women characters with a feminist perspective. This novel depicts the tragic life of Sita who leads a life of isolation and loneliness in her husband's house. Her unmitigated suffering drives her to a state of madness and desperation. Desai portrays her women characters as sentimental and introspective under the influence of British women novelists Meredith, George Eliot, Virginia Woolf and Richardson. The conflict between the need to withdraw in order to preserve one's wholeness and sanity and the need to be involved in the painful process of life is shown vividly in the novel.

This wavering between attachment and detachment reflects the need for a meaningful life. Psychological experiment of the writer in the novel can also be seen on the portrayal of Sita's character. Psychologists attach great significance to the parent-child relationship, because, according to them the patterning of emotion takes place particularly during childhood. They argue that the prevailing quality of the experience the child has with his parents particularly the mother during early childhood is of paramount importance. Childhood is the most formative period of one's life.Personality and socialization of the child begin in the family in the company of his parents who are the first individuals with whom the child interacts. Child learns the patterns of behavior which the parents set out to teach him in order to make him an acceptable member of the society. The emotion of the child depends largely on the quality of the emotional interaction that prevails between the child and his parents. Anita Desai's characters have strange childhood, and their experiences and interactions during this formative period when combined with their congenital hypersensitivity contribute towards their inability to establish and maintain harmonious inter-personal relationship in later life.

Anita Desai tries to show the anxiety of Sita who suffers because of her biased attitude towards life. Sita is over-sensitive who finds herself confined in the urban life after leading a carefree life in rural area under the protection of her father. The artificialities, fast pace and harshness of city life nauseate her to such an extent that she longs to go back to island where she has cherished all the delicacies of rural life and where she thinks her roots are. After being taken away from her father and her place, she feels the void and expects more love and care from her husband Raman. She feels insecure and finds everything wrong with Raman He had nothing more to give her, or he was just unaware of her needs and demands. He raised his hand and stroked Karan's hair with a gentleness she herself ached to attract, and stared at him, bored into him with her eyes, wanting and not being given what she wanted. (*Where Shall We Go This Summer* P 132)

Sita is a symbol of nature and cannot adjust with the mechanical world. She seems to be an 'odd one' where she is alienated from her family and society. She is upset by the sight of crows feeding on a young eagle. Immediately she rushes for a toy gun of Karan and uses it on the crows to keep them away fromthe poor eagle. The husband wife alienation forms the basis of the novel as Raman and Sita differ a lot in their temperaments. Sita always accuses Raman for his lack of understanding and Raman, could never understand the emotional state of Sita and he considers her deeds as immature and foolish ones. Sita appears to be a woman of contradictory thoughts. She is a woman of complex character and even Raman, her husband could not understand her. You must stay where there is a doctor, a Hospital, and a telephone. You can't go to the island in the middle of the monsoon. You can't have a baby there.(33)

Family plays a vital role in the growth and development of individual and broken homes definitely has its worse effect on an individual. Sita is one such victim who because of her bitter experiences in her childhood alienates herself from everything around her. Sita's character has been portrayed in such a way that it represents the predicament of a modern married woman in the society. She initially escapes from reality and later reconciles to the circumstances. Sita's life is re-defined in the island. She realizes that her own married life and all other relationship around her are based on a compromise in their duties and selfishness and this is the cause of ugliness, disharmony and increasing violence in life. She accepts reality of life instead of illusions. Unlike Maya in *Cry, the Peacock,* Sita comes out of her illusionary world. Maya always thinks about the childhood prophecy of disaster.

But Sita realizes her mistake in the magic island. Her voyage ends with the discovery that she has some responsibilities in her life. She also discovers her hidden aspects of her real life. So, the illusionary world gives way to her real world and her duties. Desai views through the eyes of her female protagonists that everyone has some duties or responsibilities in their life. They must accept it in any way. In fact, her visit to Manori helps Sita to fuse into one the span of present, past and future and life-span of childhood, youth and adult age. She redefines her relationship with her childhood soil, Manori. There is also a change in Sita's identity and she is redefining her relationship with her husband. She understands her husband and decides to go with him. Sita, therefore, return to the mainland with a sense of renewed awareness with reality rather than live in the illusory dream world like Manori.

Anita Desai's novels are certainly reflective of socials realities. But she does not dwell like others on social issues. She digs deep into the forces that condition the growth of a female in this patriarchal male dominated society. She observes social realities from a psychological perspective without posing herself as a social reformer. Her novels are studies of the inner life of characters and her talent lies in the description of minute things that are usually unnoticed. The researcher has chosen the Psycho Analytical Method for this dissertation because it is interesting to study how complex a human mind is and how differently different characters react to the same situation.

The interaction between past and present is a typical narrative device which Desai has used to convey the constant mental activity that characterizes human beings and also compensates for the limited external action. Sita's compromise marks a progression from Maya's insanity and Monisha's suicide, brings the narrative's philosophical approach to existence more into evidence -an approach that recommends a synthesis of emotion and intellect. Though the country has made a lot of progress, the role of Indian women in society remains only peripheral. Gender discrimination has been a universal phenomenon in human history from time immemorial. Owing to a new set of educational values and economic dependence, the position of women has certainly been enhanced and women have now certainly got a status in society. But in order to iron out the unevenness in society, they need to learn to assert their rights and shun the injustices heaped on them.

Thus the new generation of Indian women novelists advocates independence and assertiveness in women by depicting their characters as survivors who successfully bear torment both physical and emotional and raise a voice against the brutalities and violence surrounding them. They tend to rebuke the male dominating Indian society which discourages self-reliance in women and urge women to build up their fragmented lives and express their affirmation. Anita Desai's novels thus occupy a unique place in Indian English Literature as invaluable works of psychological study of Indian women's inner life from a feminist perspective along with the process of alienation they undergo as a part of their emotional and social changes, Sita too is not different though she acquires practical wisdom at the end of the novel. Desai's novels are thus a reflection of the disturbed psyche of women who are victims of alienation and male dominance. However, they find a way out by self-discovery and introspection.

III

BYE- BYE, BLACKBIRD

Indian women novelists project woman as the central figure by giving a distinct dimension to their image in the family and society. Their insight into the woman's reactions and responses, problems and perplexities and the complex working of their inner selves and their emotional involvement and disturbances enabled these novelists to succeed in presenting the predicament of women most effectively. The existential struggle to establish one's identity, to assert one's individuality, fight to exist as a separate identity, cultural conflicts, the social and economic changes, the problem of the expatriates and immigrants and the personal relationships especially between man and wife are some of the common themes that appear in the novels of Indian women novelists. We find the fullest expression of women's problems through display of various themes in the novels of Anita Desai. Indian couple, like Donne's lovers, together make a world of their own. Each is incomplete without the other. In a Hindu family no religious rite can be performed by a spouse without another. Though a man and a woman become complementary to each other through marriage, there is no certainty regarding their mutual love for each other.

Bye-Bye, Black bird(1971) Anita Desai's third novel has a different theme from the earlier novels. It explores in the main, the immigrant sensibility via a new foreign culture and the consequent problems of adjustment, belonging, roots, past etc. The novel acquires added significance as it examines the questions of east west encounters and cross cultural relationships. The novel *Bye- Bye, Blackbird* is mainly woven round two groups of characters, viz, Adit Sen, his English wife Sarah, the Indian friend Dev; and Jasbir – Mala, Sammar – Bella. If Maya suffers because of Psychological alienation, Sarah of *Bye-Bye, Blackbird* (1971) suffers because of cultural alienation. The novel portrays the problems of Indian immigrants in London. The title refers to England's bidding farewell to an Indian – a "blackbird". One is reminded of Kipling's view that the East is East and the West is West: and that the twain shall never meet. What is more significant, from a feminist perspective, is that East or West, woman is the underdog and the novel underscores this aspect as well.

Adit's wife Sarah has the most deserving claim to be the protagonist. Here Dev starts moving around in London like a tourist observing and enjoying its various attractions and allurements. He begins to undergo a slow change from Anglophobia to Anglophilia. Later Adit's attitude towards England undergoes a sea change. His Anglophilia gives way to a sudden and disturbing nostalgia for his home land. Through a few flash-backs, the readers are told about the love affair of Adit Sen with Sarah. Christine Longford, a friend of Adit, introduces Sarah to Adit in a cocktail party.

Even in the first meeting. Sarah's shyness attracts him and he chooses Sarah for company because "You re like a Bengali girl. Bengali women are like that, reserved, quiet. May be you were one in your previous life. But you are improving on it –you are so much prettiest" (*Bye-Bye, Blackbird,* P 73). Except this, nothing is known about their love affair.

After their marriage, they settle down in Clapham, a small city. Adit and Sarah have to adjust much because of their different cultures. To satisfy Adit, Sarah cooks Indian foods. But the typical Indian male-chauvinist in Adit finds pleasure in ill-treating Sarah : "These English wives are quite manageable really, you know. Not as fierce as they look – very quiet and hard-working as long as you treat them right and roar at them regularly once or twice a week" (*Bye-Bye, Blackbird, P 29*). Sarah, as a typical submissive wife, on the other hand, always speaks good of her husband. She pretends that she is treated nicely by her husband. When Sarah's Mother asks about her cooking, she says: "Adit Still does most of it" (P 133).

Explaining the cultural incompatibility, Krishnamoorthy Althai observes : "the rituals and beliefs of the one mean nothing to the other, which makes each of them groan in pain at the lack of regard shown by the other, for what each holds dear" (P 104). In the course of time Sarah completely alienates herself from the public and private life. In the school where she works, she avoids conversation with her colleagues who often discuss her married life. Her colleagues wonder how she is able to adjust with the Indian husband. She avoids their probing questions. She loves India. She knows something about India through the pictures of Indian stamps. She slowly changes herself. So that she can adjust with Adit's small matters. She stops cooking English food and learns to cook Indian food. After marrying Adit sen Sarah feels that she is nameless.

"She had so little command over these two canoed she played each day, one in the morning at the school and one in the evening a home, that she could not even tell with how much sincerity she played one role as the other. they were roles-and when she was not playing them, she was nobody her face was only mask, her body only a costume ..... staring out of the window at the chimneypots and the clouds, she wondered if Sarah has any existence at all, and then she wondered with great sadness, if she would ever be allowed to stop off the stage, leave the theatre and enter the real world-whether English or Indian, she did not care, she wanted only its sincerity, its truth" (P 34-35). As the "other", Sarah sacrifices a lot and she is treated like the "other" by Adit Seema Jeha looks at this predicament of Sarah from a wider perspective:" Anitha Desai draws our attention to the annihilation of self that marriage involves, for a female."(*Voice and Vision of Anita Desai, P 47*)

Adit, naturally, is a typical male-chauvinist. He never cares for his wife and her sentiments. Almost all the decisions in their family life are taken by Adit. Without consulting Sarah, he decides to return to India so that "My son will be born in India" (204). Sarah is a passive victim," the other" in the hands of the male-chauvinistic Adit, ironically, when Adit prepares himself and Sarah to leave England, Sarah gets a promotion. When Sarah informs Adit about it, Adit gets angry and accuses Sarah that she does not want to leave England whereas she has already decided not to accept promotion. The discussion leads to a confrontation and Sarah begins to weep. She seems to be more an Indian wife than a English woman. Usha Bande explains the sources of Sarah's alienation :

> "*Sarah in Bye-Bye, Blackbird is a case of both social and psychological alienation. "The social factor stems from her marriage to an Indian settled in England; her psychological trouble emanates from her pride system". (The Novels of AnitaDesai, P 119).*"

Sarah's existentialist dilemma reaches its peak at the end of the novel. Her inner conflict is the result of three problems; one pursuing Adit on his voyage to the East , second holding back to cradle and comfort the uneasy, unborn child and the third tackling the exigencies of a career that had surprisingly revealed a future. After her marriage, she has sacrificed many things to buy peace in her family life. Now she has to say good-bye to England itself where she has lived for twenty-four years.

The end of the novel suggests a peaceful conclusion: "Sarah and Adit held hands like a pair of children, feeling Bengal, feeling India sweep into their room like a flooded river ,drowning all that had been English in it"(224). In a man woman relationship there would be a need for sacrifice and surrender .But the paradox is in reality ,it is always the woman who does so. Hari Mohan Prasad compares Sarah to a volcano: "Sarah's character has more power. In her there is a real split, a real dilemma, a real suffering, but she triumphs over all these. She is a silent volcano, not dead, yet not bursting." (Journal of Indian writing in English, vol.1X No .2.P 64). The irony is Sarah never bursts in the novel. Adit, Sarah and Dev are highly sensitive and have been amenable to the sanskars of their respective root places. Adit appears to show the typical male dominant character of Indian husbands. He forgot that

Sarah was such a genuine, educated western lady, trying to cook Indian food and to please him.

Anita Desai is concerned with the delineation of psychological reality. Hence she prefers the characters who are peculiar and eccentric rather than general and common place. She conceives each character as a mystery and riddle. She believes that it is the duty of a novelist to solve this riddle. Her characters are almost sick of life and listless plaything of their morbid psychic longings. Most of her female protagonists are abnormally sensitive and usually solitary to the point of being neurotic. She was still breathing hard at having so narrowly escaped having to answer personal questions. It would have wrecked her for the whole day to have to discuss Adit with Julia, with Miss Pimm, in this sane, chalk dusted, workday office. She was willing to listen for hours to Miss Pimm's diagnosis of her aches and pains... But to display her letters from India, to discuss her Indian husband, would have forced her to parade like an impostor, to make claims to a life, an identity that she did not herself feel to be her own, although they would have been more than ready to believe her. (Bye- Bye, Blackbird. P 4)

Sarah's problem is human. She wants to be a real person whether English or Indian. She is fed –up with sitting on the fence. She tries her best to remain a sincere wife seeing to it that her marital life is not destroyed. Her husband too had been playing charade although not as consciously as she. But he also realizes falsity of his existence in England and Sarah also knows it well: "His whole personality seemed to her to have cracked apart into an unbearable number of disjointed pieces, rattling together noisily and disharmoniously" (Bye, 200). When after the 1965 Indo-Pak war Adit is in the process of making a decision to leave

England for good, he is very edgy and unstable and this is the time when he needs a cooperative and understanding wife, and Sarah does well as a wife. Of all wives in Anita Desai's novels she is the best in understanding and supports her husband.

In the circumstance mentioned above she knows how to handle her husband: She could not tell what effect the smaller refusal or contradiction might have on him. Rather she would sacrifice anything at all, in order to maintain, however superficially, a semblance of order and discipline in her house, in her relationship with him. His whole personality seemed to her to have cracked apart ... if she allowed this chaos to reflect upon their marriage, she knew its fragments would not remain jangling together but would scatter, drift and crumble.(Bye P 200)

Sarah, the English wife of Adit Sen has the same feeling of alienation as her husband. Sarah's dilemma is not that of finding new roots but it is that of uprootedness and hence deeper. She finds herself an alien and a stranger. At the time of her departure, Sarah is sad to leave her place, "It was her English self that was receding and fading and dying, she knew, it was her English self to which she must say good-bye." (Bye P 221) Like all other Desai's female characters, in this book also, treatment and domestic life of woman is the same, whether set in India or England, Desai unravels the tortuous involution of sensibility with subtlety and fineness and her ability to evoke the changing aspects of nature watched with human moods through the psychological trauma experienced by her female characters.

The main forte of Desai's fiction is the exploration of the main currents and undercurrents of human psyche. She is more concerned with the portrayal of inner reality than the outer life. The struggle of the characters, especially women, to maintain their identity and to emerge as individuals in their own right leads to maladjustment with those who are related to them. Desai's women characters are sensitive and they try their best to cope with their situation in ways that are sometimes damaging to themselves and sometimes to others, because they are often guided by impulse rather than reason. This novel deals with the treatment of the psychic tumult of her self-afflicted characters. The treatment of the characters is quite different from her earlier novels. In this novel Desai presents the typical problem of adjustment faced by black immigrants in England. She analyses this critical problem by portraying the three major characters, Adit, Sarah and Dev and exploring the effect of racial malice and hatred on their sensibility.

These three characters face the dilemma of finding their identity because their background is rooted in the different classes of society divided by birth, and from a definite sense of social placement they find themselves in an alien atmosphere where it is not easy for an individual to adjust. Anita Desai herself confesses in her article that "Their (immigrants) Schizophrenia amused me while I was with them and continued to tease me when I returned to India. I wrote it in an effort to understand the split psychology, the double loyalties of the immigrants."(Contemporary Indian Literature,XIII, 1973). After marriage Sarah's reticence turns into aloofness, she loses her zeal to participate in living and becomes apathetic. She feels that her life is an empty and ineffectual one and therefore is left with stark loneliness. Her bewilderment and frustration is the consequence of 'cultural shock'. Her immersion in a strange culture causes a breakdown in communication, a misreading of reality and inability to cope. Sarah feels depressed because she cannot fully involve herself in her husband's culture nor can she adapt herself to his society. The novelist displays commendable skill in delving deep into her psyche and highlighting her social and psychological isolation.

Sarah, like Maya and Monisha, is an introvert, but there is hardly any other kinship between them. She does not suffer from inner vacuity like them though she is temporarily isolated. Mrs. Desai's depiction of Sarah's personality, full of dualities and uncertainties, presents a vivid image of the struggles of an alienated self. Fear, insecurity and the resultant withdrawal are the three major motifs in the novel. The novel incorporates the impact of an East-West marriage on the psyche of Sarah. As the likings and tastes of husband-wife are different, a disharmony prevails in Sarah's family life and it seems to threaten her marriage. One gets the impression that Sarah and Adit have adjusted to each other despite their differences. His romantic love for England is matched with the romanticism of her imagination about India. They maintain their cultural identities yet experience a close affinity with each other's culture. But Sarah has a dread of being labelled an Indian and there in lies the crux of her difficulty.

Her sense of shame and nervousness is so obvious that some readers tend to agree with her colleague. Julia bluntly says that if being an Indian was so adherent to her, she should not have married, Sarah's irrational fear is not an out come of her social position but in the first place it is alienation only. We can analyze her motives in the light of her anxiety behind her psychological upheaval. At last we can say that *Bye-Bye, Blackbird* deals with the theme of psychological conflict encountered by the Indian immigrants in England on account of their inability to adjust with the atmosphere and situations alien to them. The novelist analyses this existential predicament by delineating realistically the situations of three major characters Dev, Adit and Sarah, who fail to come under the terms of reality and consequently feel rootless and utterly cut off from the people around them and also from their own selves.

Works Cited

Primary sources

Desai, Anita. *Bye-Bye, Black Bird,* Delhi: Orient Paperbacks, 1985.

Desai, Anita. *Cry, the Peacock.* London, Rupa Paperbacks: 1963

Desai, Anita. Where shall we go the summer - New Delhi, Vikas, 1975

Secondary sources

Baig, Tara Ali: *India's Women Power,* New Delhi, S. Chand, (1976).

Barke, G.D. "*A Study of Alienation in Bye-Bye Blackbird and The Strange Case of Billy Biswas" Critical Essays on Anita Desai's Fiction.* Ed.

Desai, Anita. "*The Book I Enjoyed Writing Most*", *Contemporary Indian Literature,* XIII, No. 4, Oct.-Dec. 1973, p. 24.

Desai, Anita. "*The Book I Enjoyed Writing Most*", *Contemporary Indian Literature*, XIII, 4, 1973.

Desai, Anita. *Bye-Bye Blackbird*, pub. Orient Paperbacks, Delhi, 1985, p. 32. 6. Ibid., p. 72.

Desai, Anita. *In Custody*. Agra: Lakshmi Narain Agarwal.1967.

Desai Anita. In Jackson Elizabeth, *Feminism and Contemporary Indian Women's Writing*. New York :Palgrave McMillan .2010.p.33

Desai, Anita. *Fire on the Mountain*, William Heinemann, London 1977: Allied Publishers, New Delhi, 1977.

Desai, Anita. *Flight of Form*, India International Centre Quarterly, Vol. 10. No. 4, D., 1982.

Desai, Anita. *The Book I Enjoyed Writing Most. Contemporary Indian Literature*, XIII, 1973. Anita Desai in her interview with Yashodhara Dalmia, *The Times of India*, Sunday Bulletin, April 29, 1979.

Deshpande, Shashi : *Literature and Gender*, Directorate of Distance Education, MDU, Rohtak, 2004.

Dubbe, P.D. "Feminine Consciousness in Anita Desai's *Fire on the Mountain*". *Critical Essays on Anita Desai's Fiction*, ed. Jaydipsingh Dodiya Pub. IVY, Publishing House, New Delhi, 2000, p. 116 &121.

Gupta, Ramesh Kumar "The Concept of New Woman In Anita Desai's *Clear Light of Day*", *Critical Essay on the Anita Desai's Fiction* ed. Jaydipsingh Dodiya Pub. IVY, Publishing House, New Delhi, 2000, p.153.

Gupta, Vijayanti : *The Guarded Tongue*, Aug. 2003,

Horney, Karan. *The Neurotic Personality of Our Time*, New York: Norton. 1937.

Iyengar, K.R. Srinivas. *Indian Writing In English*. New Delhi: Sterling Publishers, 1993.

J. Krisnamurthy : *Women in Colonial India. Essays on Survival, Work and the State*, Oxford University Press 1989.

Jain, Jasbir. *Anita Desai Indian English Novelist.* Madhusudan Prasad(Ed). New Delhi. Sterling Publishers Pvt.Ltd, 1982.

Jaydipsingh Dodiya Pub. IVY. Publishing House, New Delhi, 2000, p. 93.

Khan, M.Q. and Khan, A.G. : *Changing faces of Women in Indian writing in English*, Creative Books, 1995.

Klein, Ronald : *A Survey of Indian American Writers*, Muse India 2013.

Kumar, Ajit : *Poetic and Social Development in Indian English Poetry*, Vol. I,
Issue-II, April, 2012 www.galaxyimrj.com.

Kumar, Ashok : Portrayal of New Women – A study of Manju Kapur '*A married Women*', India Ink New Delhi, 2002, 1998, P 90.

Kurketi, Sumitra. Love Hate relationship of Expatriates in Anita Desai's *Bye-Bye, Blakbird*, the novels of Anita Desai : A critical study, E d. Bhatnagar & Rajeswar M., New Delhi: Atlantic Publishers and Distributors, 2000.

Lal, Malashri. "Anita Desai: *Fire on the Mountain*", *Major Indian Novels and Evaluations*, ed. N.S. Pradhan, New Delhi, Arnold Heinemann, 1985.

Manawat, B. Dushyant. "Ethnic Love - Hate Relationship in *Bye-Bye Blackbird". Critical Essays on Anita Desai's Fiction*, ed. Jaydipsingh Dodiya, pub. IVY, Publishing House, New Delhi, 2000, p. 93.

Monti, Alessandro and Dhawan, R.K. : Discussing Indian Women Writers : Some Feminist Issues, Prestige Books, New Delhi, 2002.

Mukherjee, Meenakshi. "A Review of *Clear Light of Day*", *The Hindustan Times*, 8th Dec., 1980.

Mukherjee, Meenakshi. "The Theme of Displacement In Anita Desai And Kamla Markandaya", *World Literature Written In English*, 17, No. 1, April 1978, pp. 225-33&240.

Parghi, Raju : Indian Drama and the Emergence of Indian Women Play-Wrights :

A Brief Survey, Impressions (e-journal) Vol. IV, Issue II, July, 2010.

Ram Atma."Anita Desai: The Novelist who writes For Herself", An Interview by Atma Ram. *The Journal of Indian Writing in English*. Vol. 5 No. 2, July 1977, p. 31.

Rana, Sunita : A Study of Indian English Poetry, International Journal of Scientific and Research Publications Vol. 2, Issue-10, Oct. 2012.

Rani, Usha. *Psychological Conflict in the Fiction of Anita Desai*, Abhishek

Publication Chandigarh, 2006, p. 15,129,203&207.

Rao, P.Malikarjuna and M.Rajeshwar. Indian Fiction in English. "*Feminism in Anita Desai.*" New Delhi: Atlantic Publishers and Distributors, 1999.

Rushdie, Salman : The Art of Critical Appreciations of Indian Novelists, Starred Reviews, London, 2008.

Sarangi, Itishri and Mukherjee, Yajnaseni : The Revolutionary Spirit of the Contemporary Women Writers of India, IOSR Journal of Humanities and Social Science Vol. 5, Issue 6 (Nov.-Dec. 2012), PP 19-21.

Saxena, Alka. "The Impending Tragedy in *Fire on the Mountain*", *Critical Essays on Anita Desai's Fiction* ed. Jaydipsingh Dodiya. Pub. IVY, Publishing House, Delhi, 2000, p. 127.

Sethi, Sunil. "Pieces of the Past: Review of *Clear Light of Day*", *India Today*, S.No. 23, Dec. 1-15, 1980.

Sharma, R.S. *Anita Desai Indian Writer Series*, Vol. 18, New Delhi, Arnold, Heinemann, 1971.

Sharma, R.S. Alienation, Accommodation and the Local in Anita Desai's *Bye-Bye, Blackbird, The Literary Criterion,* 1979.

Sharma, Ram (Dr.) : *A History of Indian English Drama,* blog posted on Jan. 24, 2010 Sunoasis Writers Network.

Singh, Kanwar Dinesh ; *Contemporary Indian English Poetry: Comparing Male and Female Voices,* Atlantic Publishers and Distributors Jan. 2008.

Szxena, Alka. "The Impending Tragedy in *Fire on the Mountain*". *Critical Essays on Anita Desai's Fiction,* ed. Jaydipsingh Dodiya Publ. IVY, Publishing House, New Delhi, 2000, p. 124.

Toffler, Alwin. *Future Shock,* London, The Bodlehead. 1970, p. 13.

Tripathi, J.P. *The Mind and Art of Anita Desai,* Bareilly, Prakash Prakash Book Depot, 1986, p. 83. [235]

Wall , Stephen. *A Neurotic Response To A Failed Marriage: George Meredith's Modern Love.* Mosaic XVII/1, winter 1984, p. 51.

Walsh, William. *The Uses of Imagination.*Desai, Anita. *Where Shall We Go This Summer*? Orient Paper backs. New Delhi: 1982. Print.[2].

Wandrekar, S. Kalpana. *The Ailing Aliens, (A Study of the immigrants in six Indian Novels),* Gulbarga, J I W E Publications, 1996.

Printed by Libri Plureos GmbH in Hamburg,
Germany